Pebble™

My World

In My
State

by Mari C. Schuh

Consulting Editor: Gail Saunders-Smith, PhD
Consultant: Susan B. Neuman, EdD
Former U.S. Assistant Secretary for Elementary
and Secondary Education
Professor, Educational Studies, University of Michigan

Capstone
press
Mankato, Minnesota

Pebble Books are published by Capstone Press,
151 Good Counsel Drive, P.O. Box 669, Mankato, Minnesota 56002.
www.capstonepress.com

1 2 3 4 5 6 10 09 08 07 06 05

Library of Congress Cataloging-in-Publication Data
Schuh, Mari C., 1975–
    In my state / by Mari C. Schuh.
    p. cm.—(Pebble Books. My world)
    Includes bibliographical references and index.
    ISBN 0-7368-4240-3 (hardcover)
    ISBN 0-7368-6118-1 (softcover)
    1. California—Juvenile literature. 2. U.S. states—Juvenile literature. 3. United
States—Juvenile literature. I. Title. II. Series: My world (Mankato, Minn.)
F861.3.S38 2006
979.4'054—dc22   2004030041

Summary: Simple text and photographs introduce basic community concepts related
to states including location, places in a state, and differences between states.

Note to Parents and Teachers

The My World set supports national social studies standards related
to community. This book describes and illustrates states. The images
support early readers in understanding the text. The repetition of
words and phrases helps early readers learn new words. This book
also introduces early readers to subject-specific vocabulary words,
which are defined in the Glossary section. Early readers may need
assistance to read some words and to use the Table of Contents,
Glossary, Read More, Internet Sites, and Index sections of the book.

Table of Contents

4

My State

I live in California.
California is a state.
It is part of the
United States of America.

The United States has 50 states. Three other states touch California.

California

- Eureka
- Chico
- Sacramento ★
- San Francisco
- Santa Cruz
- Fresno
- Bakersfield
- Pasadena
- Los Angeles
- Blythe
- San Diego

States have many
towns and cities.
I live in Sacramento.
It is my state's capital.

Places in My State

My state has many
mountains and beaches.
My state is near
the ocean.

My state has forests.
Many animals live
in my state's forests.
Grizzly bears are
the state animal.

My state has
big cities.
Millions of people
live in my state.

Other States

Some states have lots of farmland and few cities. They do not have as many people as my state.

Farmers in different states grow different foods.
Workers in some states make clothes.
Others make cars.

How is your state different from my state?
How is your state the same as my state?

Glossary

beach—an area with sand or small rocks where land meets water

capital—the city where the state's government is based

city—a big town where many people live in a small area

ocean—a large body of salt water

state—an area of land with borders you can only see on a map; each state can make some of their own laws; the United States of America has 50 states.

state animal—an animal chosen by the state government as a symbol of the state; the grizzly bear is on California's state flag.

Read More

Bruun, Erik A. *California.* State Shapes. New York: Black Dog & Leventhal Publishers, 2001.

Rondeau, Amanda. *Do Something in Your State.* Do Something About It! Edina, Minn.: Abdo, 2004.

Schroeder, Holly. *The United States ABCs: A Book about the People and Places of the United States of America.* Country ABCs. Minneapolis: Picture Window Books, 2004.

Internet Sites

FactHound offers a safe, fun way to find Internet sites related to this book. All of the sites on FactHound have been researched by our staff.

Here's how:

1. Visit *www.facthound.com*
2. Type in this special code **0736842403** for age-appropriate sites. Or enter a search word related to this book for a more general search.
3. Click on the **Fetch It** button.

FactHound will fetch the best sites for you!

Index

Word Count: 137
Grade: 1
Early-Intervention Level: 11

**LONE PINE
MEDIA CENTER**

Editorial Credits

Heather Adamson, editor; Juliette Peters, designer and illustrator; Jo Miller,
    photo researcher; Scott Thoms, photo editor

Photo Credits

Bruce Coleman Inc./Peter French, 10; Julie Eggers, 20 (background)
Capstone Press/Karon Dubke, cover, 1 (foreground), 4 (foreground), 6, 20 (foreground)
DAVID R. FRAZIER Photolibrary, 16, 18
Grant Heilman Photography/Photo Network/Howard Folsom, 4 (background);
    Chad Ehlers, 14
The Image Finders/Bachmann, 1 (background)
Photodisc, 12

The author dedicates this book to Evelyn and Moses Dolan of Lucan, Minnesota.